OOL CARS

KOENIGSEGG REGERA

BY KAITLYN DULING

EPIC

BELLWETHER MEDIA ››› MINNEAPOLIS, MN

EPIC BOOKS are no ordinary books. They burst with intense action, high-speed heroics, and shadows of the unknown. Are you ready for an Epic adventure?

This edition first published in 2023 by Bellwether Media, Inc.

No part of this publication may be reproduced in whole or in part without written permission of the publisher. For information regarding permission, write to Bellwether Media, Inc., Attention: Permissions Department, 6012 Blue Circle Drive, Minnetonka, MN 55343.

Library of Congress Cataloging-in-Publication Data

LC record for Koenigsegg Regera available at: https://lccn.loc.gov/2022044244

Text copyright © 2023 by Bellwether Media, Inc. EPIC and associated logos are trademarks and/or registered trademarks of Bellwether Media, Inc.

Editor: Rachael Barnes   Designer: Jeffrey Kollock

Printed in the United States of America, North Mankato, MN

TABLE OF CONTENTS

KING OF THE CARS	4
ALL ABOUT THE REGERA	6
PARTS OF THE REGERA	12
THE REGERA'S FUTURE	20
GLOSSARY	22
TO LEARN MORE	23
INDEX	24

KING OF THE CARS »

Cars speed down the racetrack.
One stands out from the crowd.

The Koenigsegg Regera is powerful. It has a style all its own. Some call it the king of the cars!

AUTO ROYALTY

In Swedish, regera means "to rule." That makes the Regera royalty!

ALL ABOUT THE REGERA »

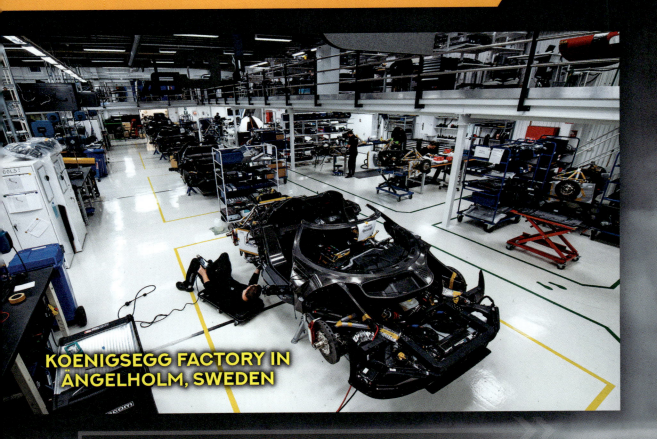

KOENIGSEGG FACTORY IN ÄNGELHOLM, SWEDEN

Koenigsegg Automotive started in Sweden in 1994. They are known for making beautiful, fast sports cars.

The CCXR and Agera are well-known **models**. Koenigsegg makes many of their own car parts!

AGERA RS

📍 WHERE IS IT MADE?

ÄNGELHOLM, SWEDEN

EUROPE

The Regera was first shown in 2015. Only 80 were made. It was the company's first **hybrid** car. Each Regera is **custom-made**. Owners choose colors, wheels, and more.

REGERA AT THE 2015 GENEVA INTERNATIONAL MOTOR SHOW

REGERA BASICS

YEAR FIRST MADE	2016
COST	starts at $1.9 million
HOW MANY MADE	80

FEATURES

hybrid twin-turbo V8 engine

wing

Koenigsegg Direct Drive

The Regera was a hit! All 80 cars were sold in around two years.

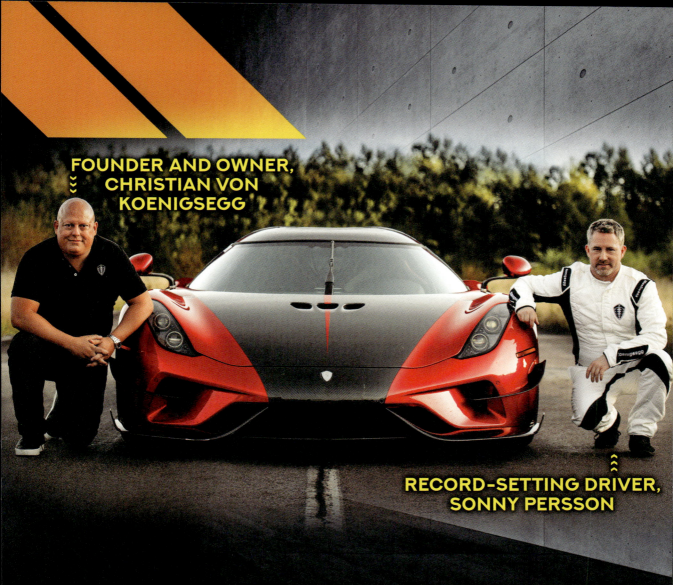

FOUNDER AND OWNER, CHRISTIAN VON KOENIGSEGG

RECORD-SETTING DRIVER, SONNY PERSSON

In 2019, the Regera set a world record. It reached its top speed and stopped again in 31.49 seconds!

PARTS OF THE REGERA ≫

Three **electric motors** and a **V8 engine** power the Regera. They work together to produce 1,500 **horsepower**!

The Regera has no **transmission**. Instead, Koenigsegg invented Direct Drive. It sends power to the rear wheels.

🔧 ENGINE SPECS

HYBRID TWIN-TURBO V8 AND THREE ELECTRIC MOTORS ≫

TOP SPEED — 249 miles (401 kilometers) per hour

0–60 TIME — 2.5 seconds

HORSEPOWER — 1,500 hp

AS SEEN IN

The Regera has appeared in many video games. Players can drive the Regera in Need for Speed games, Forza games, and more!

The Regera's body is made of **carbon fiber** and **Kevlar**. It is lightweight.

CARBON FIBER

SIZE CHART

WIDTH 80.7 inches (205 centimeters)

This car is made for speed! Its body is **aerodynamic**. A foldable **wing** sits on the rear.

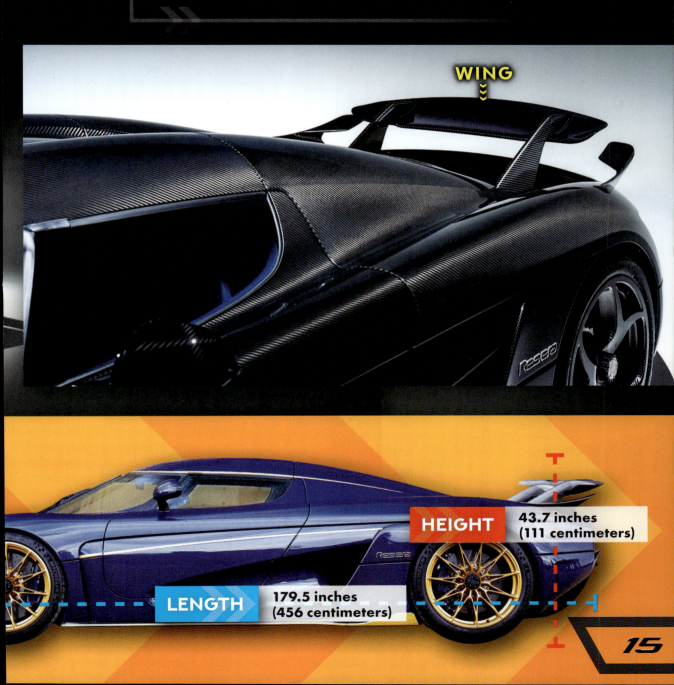

Inside, the Regera is quiet and comfortable. Direct Drive makes the ride smooth. The car starts and stops easily.

The car looks and feels expensive. Its soft seats come in many colors.

CONVERTIBLE

The Regera is a **convertible**. Its roof comes off!

The Autoskin feature makes the Regera seem like a robot. A **remote control** key opens the doors, hood, and trunk. It moves the wing, too!

PARTY IN THE FRONT

The Regera has a trunk in the front instead of the back. Some people call it a "frunk"!

TRUNK

19

THE REGERA'S FUTURE ≫

Koenigsegg stopped making the Regera. But the company is growing! They will build more cars. Soon, drivers will be able to test them on a company track.

Every Koenigsegg model has new features. Beauty and speed come standard!

KOENIGSEGG CC850

GLOSSARY

aerodynamic—able to move through air easily

carbon fiber—a strong, lightweight material used to strengthen things

convertible—a car with a folding or soft roof

custom-made—made to a particular customer's order

electric motors—parts of a car that produce power using batteries

horsepower—a measurement of the power of an engine or motor

hybrid—a car made with a gasoline engine and one or more electric motors

Kevlar—a strong human-made fiber

models—specific kinds of cars

remote control—related to a device that can control something else from a distance

transmission—a car part that shifts gears for the driver

V8 engine—an engine with 8 cylinders arranged in the shape of a "V"

wing—a part on a car's body that helps it smoothly travel through air

TO LEARN MORE

AT THE LIBRARY

Duling, Kaitlyn. *Acura NSX.* Minneapolis, Minn.: Bellwether Media, 2023.

Hamilton, S.L. *The World's Fastest Cars.* Minneapolis, Minn.: Abdo Publishing, 2020.

Swanson, Jennifer. *How Do Hybrid Cars Work?* Mankato, Minn.: The Child's World, 2022.

ON THE WEB

Factsurfer.com gives you a safe, fun way to find more information.

1. Go to www.factsurfer.com.

2. Enter "Koenigsegg Regera" into the search box and click 🔍.

3. Select your book cover to see a list of related content.

INDEX

aerodynamic, 15
Ängelholm, Sweden, 6, 7
Autoskin, 19
basics, 9
body, 14, 15
carbon fiber, 14
colors, 8, 17
convertible, 18
Direct Drive, 12, 16
electric motors, 12
engine, 12
engine specs, 12
history, 6, 8, 11
hybrid, 8
inside, 16, 17
Kevlar, 14
Koenigsegg Automotive, 6, 7, 8,
  12, 20
models, 7, 20

name, 5
racetrack, 4, 20
remote control, 19
roof, 18
sales, 10
seats, 17
size chart, 14–15
speed, 4, 6, 11, 15, 20
style, 5
trunk, 19
video games, 13
wheels, 8, 12
wing, 15, 19
world record, 11

The images in this book are reproduced through the courtesy of: Koenigsegg, front cover, pp. 7, 9 (isolated, wing, drive), 10, 11, 14, 15 (wing), 17, 20; Aab254, p. 3; Uwe Deffner/ Alamy, p. 4; CJM Photography/ Alamy, p. 5; JONATHAN NACKSTRAND/ Getty Images, p. 6; Dong liu, pp. 8-9; Joel Imanuel/ Alamy, p. 9 (engine); classic topcar, p. 12; Ank Kumar, p. 13; Composite_Carbonman, p. 14 (carbon fiber); Alexandre Prevot, p. 14 (width); Martyn Lucy/ Getty Images, p. 15 (length); Drifta Beatz/ Flickr, p. 16; pbpgalleries/ Alamy, p. 18; Grzegorz Czapski, p. 19; Jack Skeens, p. 21.